Mary Magdalene
*a disciple and friend
of Jesus*

**by
Bonnie Ring**

Jesus grew up in Nazareth, with his parents, Mary and Joseph.

When Jesus became an adult, he learned that his cousin, John was telling people to repent and then, baptizing them in the waters of the Jordan River.

Jesus went to John to be baptized.

When Jesus came up from the water, after John baptized him, the Spirit of God appeared as a dove and landed on Jesus. A voice said, "This is my beloved child, with whom I am well pleased."

After John was arrested and killed, Jesus started his own ministry.

Walking along the shore of the Sea of Galilee, Jesus called 2 brothers, Simon Peter & Andrew. They were fishermen who were casting their nets into the sea.

Jesus said to them, "Follow me and I will make you fish for people."

Jesus called 10 more men and named the 12 of them his Disciples. They were also called his 12 Apostles.

They travelled along with Jesus as he taught throughout the region of the Galilee, cured people of their diseases and proclaimed the coming of God's reign. Jesus taught his disciples, when he was not helping others.

Many women heard Jesus teach and watched him care for people and heal them.

Mary Magdalene was one of the women who listened to Jesus and she joined him and travelled with him and his disciples.

13

These men and women were with Jesus because they valued his teachings and were awed by his healings.

Often the men misunderstood or questioned Jesus. Mary Magdalene showed that she grasped what Jesus meant more than any of the others.

15

As the fame of Jesus increased, the religious leaders got angry because Jesus was doing what they believed only God could do. They plotted to have him killed, saying to one another, "It is not God who directs him, but Satan, the Evil One."

Jesus told his disciples, "the religious leaders are so opposed to me, they are going to seize me and have me killed." None of the men believed him. But when Mary Magdalene heard him speak those words, she believed that he was going to die just as he said.

When Jesus had dinner with his male disciples at Simon's house, a woman appeared whom many believe was Mary Magdalene. She broke open a white jar of costly perfumed oil and poured all the oil over the head of Jesus.

21

Some men criticized her, saying, "she could have sold that expensive scented oil for a lot of money to be given to the poor."

But, Jesus praised her and said, "Let her be. She is performing a good service for me. She is anointing my body before its burial. Truly, wherever the good news is proclaimed in the whole world, what she has done, will be told in remembrance of her."

Like the prophets who anointed kings, she was anointing Jesus to show that he was the Messiah, the Anointed One of God.

Then, Jesus took his followers to Jerusalem to celebrate the Passover. Again, Jesus warned his disciples that he would be killed.

Judas Iscariot, a Disciple, betrayed Jesus and led soldiers to arrest him and they took him to the religious leaders who opposed him.

25

The Religious leaders took Jesus to be tried by Pilate, the Roman Governor who ruled over Palestine where Jesus lived.

The crowd watching the trial became unruly. They yelled that Pilate should crucify Jesus. Afraid the crowd would riot, Pilate agreed and sentenced Jesus to death on a cross on a hill above Jerusalem.

All the male followers of Jesus ran away and hid out of fear. But, his women friends stood near the cross and watched Jesus die. Mary Magdalene was among them.

The women watched while Jesus' dead body was taken down from the cross and wrapped in a cloth to be hurriedly placed in a cave before the Sabbath began. The Sabbath was a day of rest when no work could be done.

31

Mary Magdalene and some other women observed where Jesus' body was placed in the cave, so they could return after the Sabbath to bury him properly.

At dawn on Sunday, Mary Magdalene and some other women went back to the cave to anoint the body of Jesus and bury him. They discovered an empty cave; the body of Jesus was not there.

33

An angel greeted the women and said that Jesus had been raised from the dead. The Angel said, to Mary, "go tell the disciples that Jesus has risen and that he will meet them in Galilee."

35

Feeling fear and joy, the women ran to tell the disciples. Suddenly, Jesus appeared in front of them. Jesus called Mary by name and told her, "Go tell the disciples, that I have risen and I will meet them in Galilee."

37

When Mary Magdalene reached the male apostles, they did not believe her. They only believed when they saw the empty tomb themselves.

Because she was sent to them, Mary Magdalene is called "the Apostle to the Apostles."

Mary Magdalene is an example of a good friend, because she supported Jesus during his lifetime, as he was dying and again, after he died. She understood him, valued him and offered him her friendship.

Think of yourself, are there ways that you are a good friend to your friends?

How might you also be a good friend to Jesus, now, in your life?

Jesus loved his friends, You are one of his friends and he loves you too.

48

Become a friend of Jesus today and every day, just like Mary Magdalene.

About the Author

Bonnie Ring grew up in midtown Manhattan. Shortly after her birth, she was placed in the hands of a caring young Irish Catholic Nanny whose job was to care for Bonnie and her sister who was 15 months older while their parents worked. They lived on East 79th Street close to Central Park where she played on the swings and see-saw and rode her tricycle. Mary was attentive and taught her skills which made her independent like tying her shoe laces and buttoning her shirts. Occasionally Mary took Bonnie and Star to church with her at St Ignatius of Loyola Catholic Church where Bonnie discovered a piety and prayer life that appealed to her.

From K-8th grade, both girls attended Public School 6 which was a six block walk from their home. After Mary married a man she met at Church, the couple decided to end their relationship with Bonnie's family. Bonnie was not informed of this plan until the day she left. It broke her heart to become suddenly separated from her best friend. Because she was very bright, when P S 6 created a special program for intelligently gifted children, she was placed in that class. The IG class as it was called emphasized discussion and reflection rather than memorization. She remained with that group for 4 years until all the students were merged into classes of about 30 in the eighth grade in a new building on 82nd street.

Bonnie was in the first graduating class from the new school. During the summers Bonnie attended a girls' camp in New Hampshire with her same aged cousins. Both Star and Bonnie attended the Dalton High School, a progressive independent girls' school. During her first year, Bonnie's class in Social Studies focused on the development of Western Civilization and in the Spring, her class spent an overnight at a Roman Catholic Convent. The chapel setting reminded her of her time with Mary at St Ignatius Loyola. When the priest said that God was waiting to welcome her home, she believed him and formed a renewed connection with God that was very meaningful to her.

A friend introduced her to the Church of the Heavenly Rest near Dalton where she was baptized and confirmed at age 18. She became an active member of Canterbury at Vassar College and spent the summer following her first year as a member of the summer staff of the Lower East Side Mission of Trinity Parish where she experienced God's all-inclusive love in a community for the first time. The next year she co-chaired the first inter-racial and inter-regional Episcopal Youth Conference in Williamsburg Virginia and later that year was one of 3 women founders of the Episcopal Society for Cultural and Racial Unity. She served as their first office secretary in Atlanta

Georgia and on her evenings and weekends assisted SNCC, the Student Non-violent Coordinating Committee and the Atlanta Student Movement. She completed college at New York University and enrolled in a masters and doctoral program in Adult Education at Boston University which focused on developing self-understanding and building community. Bonnie's career included 7 years as a Counseling Psychologist at UC Santa Cruz and UC Irvine. After becoming Licensed as a Psychologist, she opened a private practice first in San Francisco, then Berkeley and now in Half Moon Bay. She was the first on air psychologist in the Bay Area on KSFO radio, hosting the Dr. Bonnie Ring Show where listeners were encouraged to share their concerns and offer help to one another. As it became clear to Bonnie, that her therapeutic work was a form of ministry, she accepted a call from God to enter seminary and became ordained in the Episcopal Church. During Seminary, she became acquainted with the Women who knew Jesus as recipients of his teachings and healings, which led her to lead interactive and self-reflective retreats on those women throughout the United States and Canada that eventually led to the publication of a book, Women Who Knew Jesus. Mary Magdalene, a Disciple and Friend of Jesus is her first children's book because young girls need to know her as a role model for a life of faith.

www.ingramcontent.com/pod-product-compliance
Lightning Source LLC
Chambersburg PA
CBHW040245150626
46547CB00041B/2872